Meaningful Mourning

Ways to Celebrate the Life of a Loved One

I0173120

Dedication

This book is dedicated to all of our family members and friends who have gone on before us. We miss you.

Acknowledgment

Thanks for all of the support that was given by everyone who was involved in the writing of this book. I couldn't have done this without you.

Table of Contents

Introduction

I am writing this book as a daughter, mother, sister, and aunt. It has been developed from life experiences and is written from a personal, not professional, perspective. Like many, I have lived through tremendous grief. Grief that has brought me to where I am today.

My family is a large one. When my parents married in 1947, who could have predicted they would have 10 children, 23 grandchildren, and 31 great-grandchildren with more on the way. Our lives have been full and rich with celebrations. However, like many families, we have not been untouched by loss and tragedy. In reflecting on the loss of our family members and friends who are close to the family, I realized that we have kept the memories of those we love alive through our thoughts and actions. There are: my two sons, Todd, my firstborn child who lived a very short but meaningful life, and Josh, whose big heart failed unexpectedly at the age of 42; my niece, Jordan, who, along with her best friend, died a tragic death at the age of 15 in a single-car accident; my nephew and his wife, Jamie and Ann, who unbelievably died while in their mid-thirties from entering a well that had no oxygen in it; my sister-in-law who died at the age of 58 from cancer; my step-daughter's best friend's son, Andrew, who died at the age of 18 from an accidental drug overdose; and finally, my parents who lived into their nineties, only to have my dad die from COVID and my mom from a brain tumor. I do not give you these histories for your sympathy but for you to read this book with healing from your own loss in mind. I want the focus not to be on my family and friends but on how you can move forward with your life. I want you to be able to honor and celebrate the memory of the one you loved so that you will feel whole again.

There are many different ways to celebrate or honor the life of someone we love. Right now, I am sure you are totally overwhelmed by life itself. There is no one way to mourn; we all deal with grief differently. My hope is that this book helps you as you go through your grieving process and move forward with your life.

Taking the First Steps

Where do you begin?

You are feeling a loss that is unlike anything you have ever experienced. Losing a loved one goes deep into your being. It doesn't matter if this is your first loss or one of many; you are hurting.

The services you hold for your loved one are only the beginning. Having a professional guide you through this initial part of your grief is essential. There are so many important decisions that need to be made quickly. You have to decide where your loved one will be taken. You have to decide whether they will be buried or cremated. You have to write an obituary. You have to decide about the details of the service. You have to decide what to do with any money that might be contributed. You have to decide what to do with the flowers after the service. Thank you notes will need to be written. All of this on top of the loss of someone you love. It is overwhelming. No one should have to go through this. But you do. And, you make it.

Stories are Important

Our lives are made up of short stories that become our legacy.

From the beginning, the stories you share bring comfort. Before writing this book, I didn't know there was extensive research behind this. I now understand that we do it to keep the memories alive, even though our loved one is no longer here.

Stories matter. When my son, Todd, died at eighteen months, there were no happy stories to tell. As a medically fragile child, he had never even smiled. His short life consisted of constantly holding him in my arms and rocking him, feeding and caring for his needs, and knowing that I would never get to watch him grow old. Perhaps this is why I thought I had to put his pictures away. However, by doing this, I denied myself the grieving that I needed to go through. I denied myself the stories that should have been told, even though they were not happy ones. They were his stories, and they mattered.

The service for your loved one is a great place to start the storytelling. This allows all of the people who are sharing in your loss to grieve in a healthy way with you. The stories told at Josh's service gave his wife and daughters new memories of him at a time when they needed them most. They gave me a window into his life that I had not had as his mother. They gave my daughter a reason to smile. They gave new memories to all of us, something we so sorely needed at the time.

Unfortunately, because COVID was running rampant in our country, we could not have a service for my dad. We still needed to tell the stories. My family started them while he lay dying in the hospital. We used Zoom to share stories of our youth with our dad while he was still with us and then used Zoom to share stories of Dad after his passing. Many stories have since been added in group texts between the siblings and cousins. Stories matter, regardless of how they are told.

My mother joined my father almost two years after his passing. This time, family stories were shared at the service. The pastor gathered them in the days preceding Mom's service and made it possible for them to not only be shared with the family but friends as well. The stories shared were not new to any of us, but they were her stories that made us who we are today. Our family dynamics shifted with her passing, which made the stories even more important.

Writing allows you to share the stories over time. We have a memory jar given to me on my birthday from Josh's wife, Laura, and their daughters, my granddaughters, Carly and Taylor. The memory jar came with tickets for jotting quick notes to share at another time. We have added notecards for those who chose to write more. Carly and Taylor love hearing the stories that have been written about their dad on the tickets and notes. I remember sitting and listening to Amy tell some of the stories about her brother to the girls while they were listening in on FaceTime. No two children could have been more excited to hear new stories from their father's past. This memory jar has served us well in keeping the memories of Josh alive.

Personal Belongings

Give yourself permission to grieve.

Going through all of your loved one's possessions is heart-wrenching. After losing my 42-year-old son, Josh, we had to go through all his personal items quickly so his family could move to a new location. It is nice if you can complete this in your own timeframe, but not always practical or possible. What is important is to involve anyone who wants to be a part of this process. My 12-year-old granddaughter chose to be part of this, while her 9-year-old sister chose not to. It was too much for someone so young. It was an honor to be able to provide the stories to Carly behind many of the items Josh had kept during his life. We sorted into three piles: (1) items for the girls that would be stored in cases until the girls were in their own homes; (2) items for use in our ongoing celebration of the life of Josh; and (3) items that we would release for donation.

—

When Jamie and Ann died, my brother boxed up all of his son's books, tools, and woodworking materials and took them to his home. For the next few years, when we would ask Bill what he was reading, it was usually one of the books from Jamie's collection. He also spent hours in the shop building new memories for the kids from the wood that he had saved from Jamie's shop. The connection for him was meaningful and strong. He is also the keeper of these items for Jamie's children. He knows that there will come a time when they might want these associations with their dad, and so he is holding them for that day. I am doing the same for my granddaughters.

The difficult decisions made at this time are important at many levels. What you choose to save matters. When young children are involved, it is important to consider what these items might mean to them. Holding onto them until they are ready for them is helpful in the healing process at so many levels. Jane, mother of Ann and mother-in-law to Jamie, shares this so well in her own reflections on her loss. *"I see expressions of both their parents when I look at them, and often remind them of things their parents were good at or things they said or did. When they visit me, we often spend time going through old pictures so we can keep their first parents close in their minds and hearts. I have shared things that belonged to their parents with each of them, giving them to keep when they reached an appropriate age."*

Memory Clothing

There's nothing like being wrapped in the warmth of a memory.

Save the shirts! It doesn't matter if it's a dress, casual, or t-shirt; a special quilt or item can be made out of them. If you are lucky enough to have a family of quilters, all the better. If not, there are people out there who will be happy to help you with your memory quilts. After the death of Josh, my sister made quilts from his favorite t-shirts for his daughters. She also made a quilt for his sister, while my mother made one for each of my grandsons, Josh's two nephews. One of my special memories is when my granddaughters and I took his t-shirts and made a quilt for their mother. This was made more with love than expertise, but the love made it all the more special.

We all selected one shirt of Josh's that we wanted to keep for ourselves. For the first year after his passing, it was not unusual to see his shirts being worn by his wife, daughters, my daughter, her sons, and me. We all clung to the scent that remained of him and the loved feeling of being wrapped in his shirts. The shirts were our security blankets and still are when we need that hug that we so miss. I have two set aside to give to Carly and Taylor at a later date. We never stop needing the sensory fulfillment that comes from the possessions of someone we have lost.

Even the buttons from the shirts of your loved ones can be put to use! When my sister, Judy, was cutting up the shirts for the quilt pieces, she saved all of the buttons from them. After asking the girls if they would like to have them, I placed them in votive cups that could go on the dressers in their bedrooms. They added their own touch to this when they placed the small sealed bottles that had Josh's ashes on top of the buttons in the votives.

—

Jordan's mother, Julie, made each of the girls a memory quilt from Jordan's clothes. She threw caution to the wind and mixed t-shirts with cloth shirts. She even included the jeans pockets! Right after she passed, Julie laid out some of Jordan's clothes and had her friends come and select t-shirts they might want to take or have Julie make into pillows. Julie also saved her jewelry. Later, these pieces were worn at her sisters' and friends' weddings and to places Jordan had previously been familiar with. Julie quietly brings Jordan with her to family gatherings, making sure she continues to have her be a part of their lives.

—

Neckties can also be put to good use. They make great wall hangings! They can be sewn together or rolled and placed in square window wells so the ties are still preserved but on display to honor the professional life of someone you loved. I have also seen them framed individually. If your loved one was a professional who wore ties daily, what a meaningful way to add to a grouping on the wall that is all about them!

The Ashes

"This is my Dad." Carly

When my husband brought Josh's ashes into our house from the funeral home, he handed them to my son's oldest daughter. She opened the box and removed the bag, touching the ashes through the plastic. Her first words were, "This is my dad." I thought my heart would break. It didn't. Sometimes you need to view life from the perspective of the children who have lost the most. I knew that it was my job to be strong. I knew that it was going to be never-ending. I knew then that we would celebrate Josh every chance we had.

—

When my step-daughter's best friend, Stephanie, lost her 18-year-old son to an accidental drug overdose, I am sure she also thought her world would end. It didn't. Stephanie tells of the packets that she makes at the request of the many people who were touched by Andrew's life. In the package, she includes a few ashes, an "IT'LL BE FINE" stone, a photo of Andrew, and a little message written by her. Andrew's ashes and stones are all over the United States, Germany, Mexico, Australia, Costa Rica, the Dominican Republic, China, Egypt, and Aruba.

—

As you decide what to keep when you are sorting through all of the personal belongings of your loved one, in addition to asking yourself what you would like to keep, you could also ask yourself what best represents their life. These are the items that are meaningful to use with their ashes or in a part of your house where you memorialize them. I wish I could describe the feelings I get when I touch an object that might have been in Josh's workshop or one that he made with his girls. I feel a connection. I feel like Josh is still here. That's the feeling I wish for you.

—

Jordan loved flip-flops, cherries, and jungle prints. Julie is always in search of the flip-flops and cherries to use as decorations at the cemetery and for the holidays. The quilts and pillows that she has made over the years often include the use of jungle prints for the back.

—

Josh loved the critters his entire life. I'll never forget the day his lizard, Gary, arrived by mail along with the first supply of mealworms. Gary wasn't the first of the critters, nor the last. Over the years, he had the devotion of three cats, four dogs, one rabbit, and one frog. We now decorate his area with all kinds of critters. When I travel, I look for the perfect lizard to either put in his area or give to the grandchildren. The critters make us all smile.

The Cemetery

The grave site can represent the personality of our loved one.

My niece, Jordan, was only 15 when she and her best friend were tragically killed in a single car accident. Her parents and siblings found numerous ways to honor her that have endlessly showered Jordan with the love she generously gave to others throughout her life.

Jordan's grave is continuously decorated as the seasons change. You might find anything from a Valentine's theme to a Fourth of July decoration at her gravesite. One year it was flip-flops; the next, softball themed in the school colors of red, white, and black, and even cherry themed for her love of the cherry decorations. Her site remains as beautiful and colorful as Jordan was in life.

—

My parents' grave is shaded by a large tree in a rural cemetery. They chose the perfect place to be laid to rest together. When we were going through some of their memorabilia after Mom's passing, we came across the wedding cake top used throughout the 72 years of Mom and Dad's lives together. Something tells me it will become a part of the decorations placed so lovingly on their gravesite.

Symbols

It's the little things that matter.

Watching the birds that come to your home to find food or build their nests is comforting. It's especially meaningful when Amy and I are talking on the phone, and a cardinal appears during our conversation. It is like Josh is joining us. The same goes for the bluebirds that come into view. They make me think of my dad. My oldest brother talks of the tree frogs that hang out at his house and how much they represent Jamie. My other brother talks about the bush full of goldfinches that settled on a clump birch outside of their back door the day after Jordan's passing. My friend, Stephanie, talks of the dragonfly that has become a symbol of Andrew's presence. For me, the hummingbird has now become symbolic of my mom, always busy and moving.

—

We all have connections with nature that bring our loved ones back to us. We all look forward to the days when we just know they are reaching out to us and saying, "Hello, I'm still here for you."

Ornaments

Make new memories.

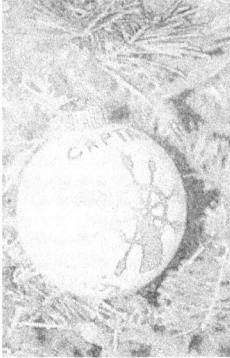

One of the most meaningful things our family did together after the loss of Josh was to celebrate him through special Christmas ornaments. Depending on the time of your loss, these can be made for Christmas, Valentine's Day, or any holiday you choose. The time spent making these becomes another opportunity for storytelling and celebrating the one you love with tears and laughter.

Following is how we made our ornaments.

- Materials for the ornament project: (1) Clear glass balls (We had two different sizes.); (2) Water-based paint; (3) Paint brushes; (4) Markers for drawing
- Instructions for the ornament project: (1) Get your materials together. Be sure to cover the surface you will be working on. This is a messy project!; (2) Start by filling the inside of the glass balls with a color or the colors you want for the inside of the glass ball; (3) Place your glass balls open side down and drain (overnight would be best); (4) Paint or draw whatever you want to commemorate the person you are celebrating on the surface of the ball; (5) Let dry and hang with a ribbon, yarn, or some type of twine, or place on a tray for display.

The best part of making the ornaments is the memories that return each time you bring them back out. Memories not only of your loved one but also of decorating them together and all of the love shared at that time. New memories are special, too.

Yard ornaments that were a part of your loved one's life are also meaningful reminders. In my home, you will find an assortment of frogs, toads, and turtles from Josh's home or rabbits that came from my parents' flower garden. I know that Jamie and Ann left a lot of yard ornaments behind that quickly became prized possessions of family members. It is surprising how many unexpected items become treasured memories from your loved ones' lives.

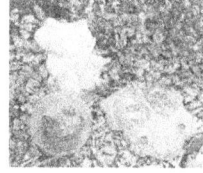

—

I will share Jane's use of the yard ornaments in her own words. "*The first spring after my husband died, my daughter helped me plan and create a small flower garden in his memory. I planted a few perennials making sure to include daisies since these were our wedding flowers. In between the new plants, we placed plaques and small statues that we had been given at the time of his death. My daughter had given her dad a farmer on a tractor statuette with a tiny wagon on the back for his last Father's Day. We decided to add that to the garden and put some of his boyhood marbles in the tiny wagon. The finishing touch came when I planted some small annuals in his old toolbox. Watching that garden grow and caring for those plants gave me more comfort than I can express.*

When my daughter and her husband died less than two years later, I doubled the size of the garden. Now there were even more precious memories to preserve. I incorporated things I had gleaned from

their garden when I was preparing their property to be sold. These included an antique pump, two teapot planters, and two little ceramic pairs of boots that I know represented their children to them. Every year I plant the teapot planters and take them and the boots to the graveside for Memorial weekend. Then I bring them home and put them back in the garden where they comfort me for the whole season.

Over the years, I have added other meaningful plants and items as I come across them. One year I added my daughter's childhood wagon and filled it with small ceramic animals that she had kept on her shelf in her room as a child. Another year I added her childhood watering can, hanging it from the antique pump that had been theirs.

While spending time in my garden, I feel a special closeness to my husband as well as my daughter and son-in-law. I have shed many tears there but have also found a peace there that often evades me elsewhere."

—

An abundance of yard statues was given to Jeff and Julie at the time of Jordan's death. Seventeen years later, those statues have become a permanent part of the flower gardens that surround their house. When they moved from Jordan's original home, they made a heart-shaped garden that contains many of the plants that were given at the time of her passing. Sprinkled throughout the garden are also Jordan's favorite flowers, gerbera daisies in a rainbow of colors. The angel statue, hug statue, two girls on a teeter-totter, and flip-flop stepping stones may not have been a part of Jordan's life when she was alive, but they represent who she was to the many friends who thoughtfully provided them.

Establishing Memorials

"It'll be fine." Andrew

Memorials can be ongoing or brief. They can be established by providing funds, symbolic gestures, or even building structures. There is no rule on what you do to memorialize your loved one. You make the call on how you want them to be honored.

When our local zoo announced a fund-raiser for building a butterfly house, my niece, Shannon, suggested we might want to memorialize her two cousins that had passed at that time. Todd and Jordan were memorialized with brass butterflies. Every time we are at the zoo with family, we always spend a little time in the butterfly area. Over the years, It has made a nice opportunity for our 18randchilddren to learn more about their family.

—

The first thing Jeff and Julie did after Jordan's passing was to establish a scholarship fund that lasted until Jordan would have graduated from high school. I remember reading through the applications with them. What a great way to help others and yourself at the same time. The students wrote of Jordan and their memories of her as well as sharing their goals for their lives.

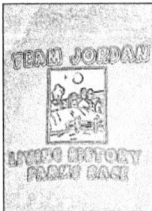

Jordan's sister, Jen, made the first memorial team commemorating Jordan in a Living History Farm's race. Close to one hundred friends and family of Jordan came to watch and participate in the race. Jen had designed shirts that were worn with pride. A lot of healing took place through the heartfelt efforts of Jordan's oldest sister.

Jordan had helped with a cheerleading camp when she was still alive. This camp has continued to this day. Her mother tells of how much it means to now see the children of the children that Jordan worked with during her short lifetime. Traditions matter.

—

Stephanie shared this in her writing about Andrew, *"About two months after his death, we worked with his friends to create a BASEketball tournament in our*

backyard. (It was the boys' idea.) If you have seen the movie BASEketball, you know it was a sports comedy disaster of a movie in the late 90's involving a made-up sport that combined baseball and basketball. His fraternity friends and other buddies came together to raise money for Andrew's memorial fund with this made-up game. It was a blast! We did this again a couple more times, but the novelty wore off quickly. The few times it did take place, I felt so much joy just being around his friends and watching them have so much fun while keeping Andrew's memory alive.

That first BASEketball tournament proved to play a much bigger role in remembering Andrew. That was the date of our first visit from

a large blue dragonfly. He stuck around and let us take photos of him as we were setting up for the tournament. Ever since then, that symbol has become one that many of us attach very strongly to Andrew. The dragonfly visits and memorial gifts from people are very special. The dragonfly lives a similar life to what Andrew's was – fast and furious and with a love of the water."

Stephanie has also found additional ways to reach out to others. Here is what she had to say. *"That first year is when we were introduced to the idea of making stones with a saying on them that reminded us of Andrew. We knew it would have to say, "It'll be fine." Andrew said that to everyone about everything. The kid just didn't let life get him down. His mantra lives on in thousands of small, blue glass stones with the words IT'LL BE FINE engraved on them. We leave them just about everywhere we go. The most fun we have with the stones is dropping them randomly on the beach, just beyond the grasp of the tides. When people walk by, we talk about if they will see the stone and if they will stop to pick it up. It's so interesting!"*

—

Josh loved the outdoors. As a child, he admired his dad for the work he did with the Department of Natural Resources. When he was little, he watched him band the ducks and geese. He met the people his dad worked with. They suggested establishing a memorial for him at one of the parks. That is what we did. Thanks to the hard work of his sister, Amy, there is now a beautiful shelter built in his honor at the park where the two of them spent a lot of time running around the lake, fishing, and hanging out together. We also added a bench at the shelter area in memory of Todd. Better late than never.

Faith

Faith provides a strength we didn't know we had.

As hard as it is to accept what has happened, faith has a way of providing a level of peace when dealing with life's sometimes cruel events. Such is the case with Jane, the mother of Ann and mother-in-law of Jamie.

Jane's faith is reflected in the following: "*Many people believe that everything that happens is God's will. That is how they handle their devastation when accidents and tragedies happen. I do not believe that God ever wills for horrible and often freakish accidents to happen that leave young parents dead and young children orphaned. I do believe that when those things do happen in this world of ours, that God sends the bereaved the people and the thoughts they need to make it through each day. As the grieving, it is our responsibility to open ourselves to these people and let God work through them. For me, it came through family, people I worked with, people in my church, friends, and sometimes even passages I would read in a novel. I learned that there were many who were grieving and that together we could make it through the process with our faith intact. Without God working through these people, I know I would have given in to despair. Instead, I feel supported and whole. I also believe in heaven. It gives me much comfort to know that I will one day again be with those I love the most, and that until then, they are aware of what is going on in my life and the lives of all who loved them.*"

Ongoing Communication

It's important to allow people who are mourning to talk.

Communication can occur at any place and at any time. For some, communication is talking. For others, communication is listening. Still, others need to do both. You have no idea how you will react when you lose a loved one. I reacted in different ways to the deaths of my two sons. With Todd, I withdrew into myself, and with Josh, I talked nonstop. Mourning is unpredictable. It is what it is.

—

The shock of hearing the news of the deaths of my nephew, Jamie, and his wife, Ann, returns each time I think about their untimely passing. The role of caring for their two young children fell upon my niece and her husband. The house had to be closed down and put on the market, and the home they were moving to had to be modified to accommodate two more children, but most important, Kennedy and Brendan needed to mentally survive this unbelievable shift in their lives. Each day, each week, each month, and each year, my niece and her husband were continuously finding ways to celebrate a mother and father who would never return. They were embracing a new world where my great-niece and nephew knew they were loved and wanted.

Their communication often took place at the dinner table. It wasn't planned, but it was encouraged. The conversations helped two young children and their young cousin keep the memories alive and hear new stories to add to their "new normal." One very special conversation came when they all decided together that their new family would be solidified through adoption. Kennedy and Brendan kept their last names to honor their first parents, but they officially recognized the parents they now have and who are raising them with so much love.

Pictures Matter

Putting the pictures away will not erase the memories.

When my first son died at the age of 18 months, I put all of his pictures away. If you didn't know me when he was alive, you didn't know I had had a child. Typical 70's style, I closed that part of my life down. I don't recommend that.

—

My brother and his family visited us in Colorado the summer after their 15-year-old daughter, Jordan, had passed in the spring. They wanted to bring her back to a place where memories had been made with her. They didn't have ashes, but they did have pictures. Her sisters had cut out her pictures and placed them on the end of tongue depressors so that she could be placed wherever they wanted. She was batting a softball in one, pitching in another, posing in a formal dress for her prom, and in her cowboy hat in another. They had captured her in some of the happiest times of the final days of her life. She went everywhere with us on that trip. She rode on the car window as we drove the mountain roads. We took her to the top of a mountain and left one of her pictures wedged in rocks overlooking a valley below. We even had her eating with us in restaurants. In

later years, "Jordan on a Stick" was even at the weddings of her cousins! What a novel idea her two older sisters had with so much love shared.

—

The feeling that comes when people send a picture that you have never seen before is one of knowing that your loved one is still thought of by others. The cell phone makes it so easy to share a photo you come across of someone who has passed on. Just take a quick picture and send it forward with a short note of the event. It's like another new memory.

—

I also love the way our phones can randomly display pictures. I look forward daily to seeing what memory will be projected on my phone as a video or picture. I often share the memories in an email or text with people who share our common memories. It makes me feel good, and I hope it does the same for the person I share it with.

Celebrate Special Occasions

We are not in the seventies. It's ok to grieve.

Birthdays are hard. Previously a time of celebrating life, it is instead a time when you celebrate how old they would be today if they had lived. It's also a time that is more personal than others.

I remember the first birthday after my oldest son, Todd, died was one filled with loneliness. I wanted others to remember this special day, but I quickly realized that it was not going to happen. I had over forty of those lonely days of remembering Todd's birthdate until I realized that by putting all of his pictures away, I had unintentionally sent out a message that I didn't want to remember. That was not the case. I never forgot. I was just unaware of how important it was to celebrate his memory with others. That is, until the death of my adult youngest son, Josh.

When the anniversary date of Josh's birthday came, I bought balloons and flowers and ensured he was honored on his birthdate. I also surrounded his ashes with artwork that his girls had made when they were young. He had asked me to save the girls' crafts when he was still alive. I had no idea then that I would be using those pieces to bring heart and love into his celebrations. Of course, I also included some critters! I love to share this time with Laura and the girls as well as Amy and family through text and pictures. As time has gone by, I have found that it's really special when we can FaceTime or Zoom and decorate Josh's area together.

A lot of thought and planning goes into preparing for his birthday celebration. The best part is it is filled with happy thoughts and good memories.

Amy and her husband, Derek, also put a lot of love into celebrating her brother's birthday. One year they sanded drywall on his birthday. The three of them spent a lot of time together working on remodeling projects, so what better way to celebrate him than with an act that would be inclusive of all of them! Of course, the day ended with roast beef, green beans, mashed potatoes, and gravy. Josh never failed to request this for his special birthday dinner, so they have now become a new food tradition for all of us on each February 12!

—

Jordan's birthday is celebrated each year through a combination of remembrances. The first year a picture board was put together with each of her 15 birthdays. That picture board has come out every year on her birthday since. The first year also included a celebration at the cemetery with balloons released by her family and young friends. In the years since, her sisters and mother also post pictures of Jordan on Facebook to commemorate her special day. Jeff and Julie always place a few key decorations at the cemetery, like a flag of the Iowa Hawkeyes, her favorite football team, and some colorful fall flowers to make the celebration of Jordan complete.

—

The birthday of Stephanie's son, Andrew, came only ten days after his death. The telling of that event can only be shared in Stephanie's words. *"Ten days after his death, his birthday arrived. He would have been 19 years old, and I couldn't imagine not celebrating, as sad and lost as I was. The family decided to invite a large group of his friends and family to a park that we had been to several times with Andrew. We often went to take pictures for homecoming, prom, etc. Everyone was invited to bring their own meal – preferably something from Taco Hut, which is what Andrew called the Taco Bell/Pizza Hut combo fast food restaurant that he and his friends frequented. I'm pretty sure I was still in shock at that time. I picked up cupcakes from his favorite spot, and we had tacos with about 20 of his friends. It was surreal to be celebrating his 19th birthday without him, but it felt like the right thing to do. I know Andrew was watching and smiling."*

—

We all have different ways of celebrating special occasions. Finding the perfect birthday or anniversary card for your loved one allows you to spend some precious time with them while looking for a card that says exactly the right thing. My sister bought a single red rose for my mom on Mom and Dad's anniversary date, Mom's birthday, and Valentine's Day and sent them from Dad. Both of them gained meaningful memories from this thoughtful act that lasted until Mom's passing.

Save Digital Documents

Take advantage of today's technology.

We are so fortunate today to have the technology we have available to us. When Todd died in 1972, I put together a scrapbook of his short year and one-half with us. Many of the photos were Polaroid (which fade over time), and others were taken with Instamatic cameras. I did my best to save the artifacts, but we just didn't have the resources back then.

Following are some ways to preserve the digital document of your loved ones.

- Screenshots of the online condolences
- Print out/save the text messaging that was sent to you by your loved one
- Scan photos...These could come up later in one of the videos your phone makes for you today!
- Make a memory book of the photos from the service.

Social media has given us a whole new window into peoples' lives. If your loved one had social media accounts, you have the added blessing of being able to look back at their lives through their postings. My niece even saved her sister-in-law, Ann's, postings from Facebook and shared them with Kennedy when she felt the time was right.

We are all so fortunate to have videos that capture our loved ones' movements and voices at different times in their lives. It is very comforting to know that we can bring back a brief time in our lives when they were still with us.

Listen to Their Music!

Savor the memories.

I became an Eddie Vedder fan after Josh's passing. I learned so much more about Josh through listening to his music. I had no idea that was why he wanted to learn to play the ukulele. I had heard him talking about getting one and had even looked at one to buy for him the summer before he died. I missed that chance. Listen to what your loved ones are telling you in their words and even in their music. Life is fleeting, and second chances don't always come around.

—

There are always memories in songs. Josh's girls light up with the songs they experienced with their dad. After Josh's death, Carly worked on a playlist of his songs. I became aware of this playlist the summer after Josh died when Carly, Taylor, my husband, and I were returning from a memorable trip to Colorado. Carly connected to the car phone and began playing her songs. The first one she played was "Chicken Train" by the Ozark Mountain Daredevils. Suddenly, the conversations became lively and filled with songs that Josh had loved. Bob and I heard fun memories about their dad. I can still see them today, filled with the animation I had missed seeing in them since Josh's passing. A new meaningful memory was made.

—

One of Jordan's favorite songs was "Fishin in the Dark" by the Nitty Gritty Dirt band. Her mother, Julie, states this song can never come on without the lively memories of Jordan. It wasn't her only "favorite." Jordan and her boyfriend also shared a song, "Two Hearts" by Zona Jones. In fact, it was one that she would sing to him. Knowing this, her sisters printed out the song for him and included it with some special pictures of their times together. This act of giving was one of meaningful mourning for all parties involved.

Cook Their Favorite Foods!

Food can't help but bring on memories.

Dinner time is such a natural time to remember our loved ones. It may be the food you are eating, a story from a time you were at the dinner table together, or a favorite food your loved one had that allows you to share stories or have meaningful memories or conversations.

I asked members of my family what foods they use to celebrate the loved ones that have gone before us. Following are some of the ways they shared.

—

For Josh, it will always be roast beef, mashed potatoes and gravy, and green beans for all of us. We also like to celebrate him with hot beef sandwiches, spaghetti (modified to his recipe), chili, Kippersnacks, apple pie, and Rolos. One of our favorite stories comes from his love of pies. It was Thanksgiving of either 1979 or 1980. Traditionally, I was the pumpkin pie baker for the family dinners, and this year was no different. I had made three beautiful pumpkin pies and placed them on the table to cool. Around 10:00 pm, I went into the kitchen to cover the pies and discovered that a big chunk of filling was gone from one of the pies. I thought the cat had done it and immediately went into a frenzy (that is mild). I sent my husband to the local gas station to pick up more pumpkin pie filling and started remaking all three of the pies.

There was no way I would take a chance on the cat having put her nose on the rest of the pies. The pies were out of the oven and ready to go around midnight that night. Flash forward thirty-plus years…Josh finally confessed that it was his finger that was put in the pie, not the cat. I guess we could add pumpkin pie to his list of favorites.

—

You don't have to cook your loved one's favorite foods to have the food memories. Julie states that Jordan was fond of the Dairy Queen. After the death of Jordan, Jeff would stop at the Dairy Queen and share that moment with Jordan before his visits to the cemetery. Jordan also loved to eat the fat off her family's steaks. Needless to say, each steak now brings about memories of Jordan. Because Jordan was still at home when she passed, they are more aware of her eating habits than her favorite foods. They are now enjoying watching their grandson, Elliott, eat pizza just like she did (peels off the topping and just eats the crust).

—

Jamie and Ann must have made a lot of chili at their house, as Jamie's chili is a favorite of Kennedy and Brendan. Jamie's dip is also high on the request list of all of the family. It is a simple combination of browned hamburger cooked with Rotel for 10 minutes, then topped with cheese. Add the chips, and everyone loves the food as well as the memories!

—

For our dad, a long list came from my nine siblings: cornmeal mush, pancakes, Braunschweiger, summer sausage, dried beef, hash, liver, ham and bean soup, oyster stew and open-faced sandwiches, anything with raisins, gooseberry pie, cream puffs, donuts, sweet potato pie, divinity, peanut clusters, chocolate covered cherries and raisins, and homemade ice cream. Also, Amy and I always think of him when we use mustard because he didn't like it! It can work both ways!!!

—

With the more recent passing of our mother, I have reached out once

again to my siblings, asking them to share their food connections with Mom. Mom was a woman who could feed all of us on a shoestring budget with foods that were pretty hard to top.

The following were shared with enthusiastic consensus: creamed (garden) peas with new potatoes, green beans from the garden, hamburger soup, vegetable soup with fresh wheat bread, open-faced cheese and bacon sandwiches, homemade stuffing (oh, the smell of the onions and celery cooking in butter), potato salad, chicken dumplings, homemade noodles with beef or chicken, her lemon Jello salad, angel food cake, apple sheet cake, all of our special birthday cakes (carrot, applesauce, white/coconut frosting), reduced sugar oatmeal raisin cookies, peppernut (Pfeffernusse) cookies, sugar cookies, Cherry Go-Round, brownie pudding, mincemeat pie, cinnamon rolls, donuts

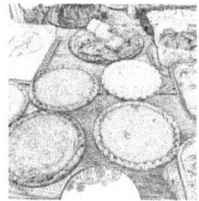

(straight out of the fryer), and PANCAKES every Saturday morning! The list could go on and on…

My brothers tell of their experiences with the food Mom sent them while they were in the military. Bill thought the pumpkin bread was a green cake, and Jeff's cookies were nothing but crumbs, but they were still enjoyed by the whole crew. Our Mom loved taking care of us with the food.

—

Cinnamon rolls were Mom's specialty. A week before she passed, I baked her some homemade cinnamon rolls using her recipe, mixer, and rolling pin. I hadn't made them since I was in my teens, but it didn't matter. Mom was thrilled to eat them and even let me know they could have used a little more cinnamon. ☺ I look forward to continuing the practice of making the rolls with Mom's recipe. I am proud to carry on that tradition.

Go to Their Favorite Vacation Spots

Traveling down memory lane takes on a whole new meaning.

If you were fortunate enough to spend time traveling with your loved one, returning to your favorite places will immerse you in memories of them.

Jeff and Julie have found ways to return to those places and continue those memories during the holiday season. Christmas trees are often themed based on the love of Jordan. Julie is good at finding and decorating with items from the places they had traveled with Jordan. I especially love the year the tree was beach-themed. Once again, the lightness and happiness of Jordan as a young girl were brought into their home.

—

Josh loved the water. He and his young family would launch their pontoon into the lake near their home and spend countless hours boating. On one of my visits after his passing, Carly and I drove to the dock by the ramp they regularly used for entry into the lake. Before getting there, she was talking about how special docks are because of all of the people they bring together. Sure enough, while we were there her former pre-school teacher and her grandson, Carly's classmate, arrived at the dock in their own boat as they were ending the day on the water. Ironically, this family was dealing with grief that was similar to ours. Carly and her classmate were connected through the loss of a parent, and I was connected to her teacher through the loss of a child. Carly was right, docks are special places for bringing people together.

—

We recently went back to a vacation spot that had originally only included Amy and Josh. No marriages had taken place yet, and no children had been born. We wanted to include Josh in some way in the canoeing trip down the river. With everyone's blessing, we each wore one of Josh's hats on our five-hour float. Such a simple but meaningful way to have him with us.

Amy also brought along a bag of Riesen candy that had a private connection for her to Josh from the first canoe trip. The two of them had run out of "beverages" on their previous trip while sharing the float down the river. They managed to raid candy out of our cooler (the Riesen's) they had never eaten before. A new taste in candy and a memory was born! Amy said it was definitely worth commemorating on this second trip!!!

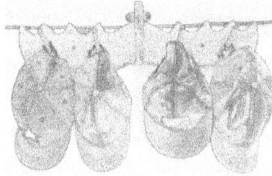

Watch Their Favorite TV Shows!

Who ever thought TV viewing could bring so many memories.

When Amy and Josh were younger, they spent hours laughing at the sitcoms that were a part of the '70s and '80s. As they became adults, I would hear them exchanging lines from those sitcoms in some of their fun and lively exchanges. Their respective spouses, Derek and Laura, quickly caught the banter and joined in the fun. They all never ceased to amaze me with the inside jokes formed during those times together.

One thing that Amy, Derek, and Laura have found comforting is rewatching some of the television shows and movies they had shared when Josh was alive. I love to hear when they have taken the time to rewatch those shows and can still share some of the time-worn jokes and lines from those special times together.

I have heard Josh's girls talk about how he would turn off a show he might be watching so they could see the one they wanted. Their memories are in recalling how he would then sit and watch the entire show they had chosen with them.

My parents will forever come to mind when I hear of the Lawrence Welk show, Molly Bee, Gunsmoke, Jeopardy, and Wheel of Fortune. Even after Dad was gone, Mom faithfully watched the Lawrence Welk show and Molly Bee every Saturday night. I can only imagine how meaningful that was to her.

39

Closing

"Grief doesn't change. You just get better at knowing what to do." Amy

We will always mourn the loss of our loved ones. It is especially difficult to lose those who leave us so early in their own lives. I hope that the ideas and thoughts I have shared with you in this short book will fill your life with anticipation of how you can continue sharing your memories in meaningful ways, both for you and others.

During the writing of my book, I reached out to family members and friends who had also known great losses in their lives. Some responded, and some chose to remain private in how they mourn the loss of their loved ones. There is no right or wrong way. We all mourn in our own ways.

Stephanie and Jane both said they found it comforting to share in writing what they had done to commemorate the lives of their children. With their permission, I have included what they wrote. I did not put everything they said into the body of this book, but feel the words and actions they shared all needed to be a part of this publication. You will find their full manuscripts in the appendix. I would encourage you to also think about writing about the different ways you have celebrated your loved one.

We all know that sorrow is not predictable. All it takes is one "trigger," and you can find yourself on the floor in a corner, crying out of control. What you feel matters. You matter. However, it is most important to give yourself permission to be happy again. This is what I think each of our loved ones would want for us. This, too, is a meaningful way to celebrate your loved one.

Appendix 1

Jane, Mother of Ann and Mother-In-Law of Jamie

There are probably as many ways of dealing with grief as there are people grieving. Some grief is normal and just part of the life process. Some are profound and shake the very core of a person's identity. Losing my only daughter and son-in-law to a country well accident when she was 34 and he was 36, still remains in the profound category for me. There were many coping mechanisms I used to get through each day. The ones I used and still use the most all start with G: God, Grandkids, Gardening, Gifting, and Gratitude.

God

Many people believe that everything that happens is God's will. That is how they handle their devastation when accidents and tragedies happen. I do not believe that God ever wills for horrible and often freakish accidents to happen that leave young parents dead and young children orphaned. I do believe that when those things do happen in this world of ours, God sends the bereaved the people and the thoughts they need to make it through each day. As the grieving, it is our responsibility to open ourselves to these people and let God work through them. For me, it came through family, people I worked with, people in my church, friends, and sometimes even passages I would read in a novel. I learned that there were many who were grieving and that together we could make it through the process with our faith intact. Without God working through these people, I know I would have given in to despair. Instead, I feel supported and whole.

I also believe in heaven. It gives me much comfort to know that I will one day again be with those I love the most and that until then, they are aware of what is going on in my life and the lives of all who loved them.

Grandkids

My grandchildren were 7 and 3 when their parents both died. When my daughter was on life support in the hospital immediately following the accident, I promised her that I would put her kids first for the rest of my life. I have truly tried to do that. The ironic thing is, they have been as much support for me as I have been for them.

I see expressions of both their parents when I look at them, and I often remind them of things their parents were good at or things they said or did. When they visit me, we often spend time going through old pictures so we can keep their first parents close in their minds and hearts. I have shared things that belonged to their parents with each of them, giving them to keep when they reached an appropriate age.

When the children come to stay with me individually, they stay in the room their mother grew up in. It is not a shrine to her; it is just a room. I do feel it gives them a sense of what her life was like when she was their age.

It is mainly because of my grandchildren that my life still has meaning.

Gardening

The first spring after my husband died, my daughter helped me plan and create a small flower garden in his memory. I planted a few perennials making sure to include daisies since these were our wedding flowers. In between the new plants, we placed plaques and small statues that we had been given at the time of his death. My daughter had given her dad a farmer on a tractor statuette with a tiny wagon on the back for his last Father's Day. We decided to add that to the garden and put some of his boyhood marbles in the tiny wagon. The finishing touch came when I planted some small annuals in his old toolbox. Watching that garden grow and caring for those plants gave me more comfort than I can express.

When my daughter and her husband died less than two years later, I doubled the size of the garden. Now there were even more precious memories to preserve. I incorporated things I had gleaned from their garden when I was preparing their property to be sold. These included an antique pump, two teapot planters, and two little ceramic pairs of boots that I know represented their children to them. Every year I plant the teapot planters and take them and the boots to the graveside for Memorial weekend. Then I bring them home and put them back in the garden where they comfort me for the whole season.

Over the years, I have added other meaningful plants and items as I come across them. One year I added my daughter's childhood wagon and filled it with small ceramic animals that she had kept on her shelf in her room as a child. Another year I added her childhood watering can, hanging it from the antique pump that had been theirs.

While spending time in my garden, I feel a special closeness to my husband as well as my daughter and son-in-law. I have shed many tears there but have also found a peace there that often evades me elsewhere.

Gifting

My daughter collected a few things during her lifetime. She loved music boxes, teapots, and Amy Andersen figurines. Most of these came to me upon her death. As months passed, I often chose one of these meaningful possessions to give to special cousins and aunts. I always presented them in a one-on-one visit, where we could share wonderful stories and memories of my daughter's life. My feeling was that everyone who kept a remembrance of my daughter and her husband in their home would keep their memories alive and share their story.

Of course, the most meaningful gifts have been the ones given to their children. By spreading them out and gifting them at appropriate times, the gifts become treasures and very meaningful to them and to me.

Gratitude

Having gratitude become a way of coping with grief came as a surprise to me. I just happened upon it accidentally. There have been so many times that something extraordinary would happen. I would get a very thoughtful card or a phone call, or someone would share a funny or touching memory. Sometimes it would be something in the garden that was especially beautiful that day or a butterfly that landed on my arm and stayed for a moment. I found myself thinking of these things at the end of the day, and I just automatically gave thanks for them. Soon it became a conscious practice. I simply take a few minutes at the end of the day to think of all that has taken place, and I always give thanks for the good that happened on that day. That gratitude has become my motivation for facing another day

Appendix 2

Stephanie, Mother of Andrew

Things we have done to celebrate Andrew – 5/31/92 – 5/21/11

In the first year, it seemed like we did so many things to remember Andrew. We couldn't get enough of creating experiences to remember him. We were grasping for ways to keep his memory alive by creating more memories of him, without him.

Ten days after his death, his birthday arrived. He would have been 19 years old, and I couldn't imagine not celebrating, as sad and lost as I was. The family decided to invite a large group of his friends and family to a park that we had been to several times with Andrew. We often went to take pictures for homecoming, prom, etc. Everyone was invited to bring their own meal – preferably something from Taco Hut, which is what Andrew called the Taco Bell/Pizza Hut combo fast food restaurant that he and his friends frequented. I'm pretty sure I was still in shock at that time. I picked up cupcakes from his favorite spot, and we had tacos with about 20 of his friends. It was surreal to be celebrating his 19th birthday without him, but it felt like the right thing to do. I know Andrew was watching and smiling.

That first Fourth of July, we all gathered at my mom's house in Mason City, where I grew up. She was living in the house where I lived when Andrew was born. We all wrote messages to Andrew on mylar balloons and released them into the sky, sending our messages high into the air, hoping Andrew would be able to find them. There is something about watching a balloon float so high that at last, you lose sight of it that feels like a connection from Earth to the heavens.

About two months after his death, we worked with his friends to create a BASEketball tournament in our backyard. (It was the boys' idea.) If you have seen the movie BASEketball, you know it was a sports comedy disaster of a movie in the late 90's involving a made-up sport that combined baseball and basketball. His fraternity friends and other buddies came together to raise money for Andrew's memorial fund with this made-up game. It was a blast! We did this again a couple more times, but the novelty wore off quickly. The few times it did take place, I felt so much joy just being around his friends and watching them have so much fun while keeping Andrew's memory alive.

That first BASEketball tournament proved to play a much bigger role in remembering Andrew. That was the date of our first visit from a large blue dragonfly. He stuck around and let us take photos of him as we were setting up for the tournament. Ever since then, that symbol has become one that many of us attach very strongly to Andrew. The dragonfly visits and memorial gifts from people are very special. The dragonfly lives a similar life to what Andrew's was – fast and furious and with a love of the water.

That first year, we were introduced to the idea of making stones with a saying on them that reminded us of Andrew. We knew it would have to say, "It'll be fine." Andrew said that to everyone about everything. The kid just didn't let life get him down. His mantra lives on in thousands of small, blue glass stones with the words IT'LL BE FINE engraved on them. We leave them just about everywhere we go. The most fun we have with the stones is dropping them randomly on the beach, just beyond the grasp of the tides. When people walk by, we talk about if they will see the stone and if they will stop to pick it up. It's so interesting!

These stones have become a part of my Andrew's Ash's package. Anyone can request a bit of Andrew's ashes to take to any destination and leave there in his memory. In the package, I include a bit of ash, an IT'LL BE FINE stone, a photo of Andrew, and a little written message from me. His ashes and stones are all over the United States and many cool places around the world, including Germany, Mexico, Australia, Costa Rica, the Dominican Republic, China, Egypt, and Aruba, just to name a few!

Many years after his death, I attended a conference about the opioid epidemic. Shortly after that, I joined the board of Coalition Rx, a local community organization. I am now the vice president of the board. Our mission is to reduce the misuse of all substances of abuse by raising awareness through education, prevention, and policy advocacy. Through this board, I have been able to talk to various groups and organizations about my loss and how to help prevent opioid abuse by locking up your medications. This opportunity gives me an outlet where I can feel like I am helping to prevent other families from this type of terrible loss.

Other ways we have remembered Andrew:
- Bracelets were made with his name on them in his memory
- T-shirts were made and worn in memory walks
- We had dog tags made with his photo on them for family members and friends

- Pillows were sewn by a friend from his old t-shirts. They were given to many friends and family
- We have gathered with his friends and family on his birthday many years and done pow-wow shots while sitting on the floor – a shot ritual he and his friends had done together with a shot consisting of red bull and Jägermeister
- Many people have tattoos in his memory – I included a photo of one that Jesslyn has
- There is a bench on the UNO campus by Andrew's dorm where he passed. It has his name on it, and his saying IT'LL BE FINE
- We have stones and a bench in our yard in his memory
- I wrote his name, and IT'LL BE FINE on a banner that went to the Olympians who were swimming for the USA
- A few of us have some version of IT'LL BE FINE on our license plates
- On his death anniversary, we go to the dorm and visit the bench. We leave behind flowers, and IT'LL BE FINE STONES. We also typically go to some of his favorite places and randomly give strangers money with a small flyer with Andrew's photo and the saying IT'LL BE FINE.
- We have donated to several causes in Andrew's memory
- There is a brick on the sidewalk in Clear Lake, IA, near a local bar that is frequented by Andrew's family
- We have made bumper stickers and window stickers that many people have on their cars